Explaining Bread and Wine

Derek Brown

Sovereign World

ISBN: 1 85240 162 1

This Sovereign World book is distributed in North America by
Renew Books, a ministry of Gospel Light, Ventura, California, USA.
For a free catalog of resources from Renew Books/Gospel Light,
please contact your Christian supplier or call 1-800-4-GOSPEL.

SOVEREIGN WORLD LIMITED
P.O. Box 777, Tonbridge, Kent TN11 0ZS, England.

Typeset and printed in the UK by Sussex Litho Ltd, Chichester, West Sussex.

Contents

1

Do This in Remembrance
of Me

"For I received from the Lord that which I also delivered to you: that the Lord Jesus, on the same night in which He was betrayed, took bread; and when He had given thanks, He broke it and said, 'Take, eat; this is My body which is broken for you; do this in remembrance of Me.' In the same manner He also took the cup after supper, saying, 'This cup is the new covenant in My blood. This do, as often as you drink it, in remembrance of Me.' For as often as you eat this bread and drink this cup, you proclaim the Lord's death until he comes."   (1 Corinthians 11:23-26 NKJV)

The reports that Paul is receiving from Corinth are not good. There are reports of immorality, believers are going to court against one another and meetings are often in total disorder. As part of that disorder, when the church comes together for the Lord's supper, the communion or the 'breaking of bread' which they ironically call the 'love feast'; believers who have plenty are looking after themselves, eating and drinking in an orgy of self-indulgence (there are even reports of some being drunk). They do not share their abundance with others who are needy and the poor look on humiliated and ashamed. Paul's reply is one of anger and rebuke. *"What! Do you not have houses to eat and drink in? Or do you despise the church of God and shame those who have nothing? What shall I say to you? Shall I praise you in this? I do not praise you."*

Before we sit back and congratulate ourselves that this doesn't happen in our churches, let us ask ourselves are we really any nearer to what Jesus meant when He gave such clear instructions concerning the Lord's Supper?

5

He intended this meal to have a powerful impact on the lives of His followers until the day that He would come again. Yet the meal usually takes place in an occasional Sunday service, and is very often added on to the end of the normal programme. Occasionally people will break bread and drink wine in a house group or at a meal, but it's safe to say that very few believers have really realised or appreciated the power and the benefits of this meal instituted by Jesus.

There is a danger in not understanding the importance of this act of remembrance. *"When you come together it is not for the better but for the worse"* (1 Corinthians 11:17 NKJV), or as the NIV puts it, *"Your meetings do more harm than good."* In other words, taking communion in the wrong spirit will leave you worse off than if you have not taken part in it. Going back to our friends in Corinth, there was a serious problem in the church of sickness, weakness and premature death. Paul put the blame for this problem on their failure to understand the full meaning of taking bread and wine: *"That is why many of you are weak and ill, and some have died"* (1 Corinthians 11:30 RSV). The Corinthian church was noted for its charismatic ministry. There was no lack of power, nor of spiritual gifts. Paul makes this clear: *"I always thank God for you because of his grace given you in Christ Jesus. For in him you have been enriched in every way – in all your speaking and in all your knowledge – because our testimony about Christ was confirmed in you. Therefore you do not lack any spiritual gift"* (1 Corinthians 1:4-7 NIV). But despite this, they were unable to prevent weakness, sickness and premature death among their members. The same can be true today. This study was born out of a question that arose in my mind when I sat with a group of Christian leaders and heard the 'casualty reports' in their churches of serious sickness, tragedy and premature death. The question was, if this is exactly what Paul spoke of – what are we missing?

According to Paul, the essential element that was lacking was not charismatic gifts or power. He had said to the Corinthians earlier in his letter, *"You come short in no gift"* (1 Corinthians 1:7 NKJV) and spoke later of the abundance of charismatic gifts in their meetings. *"How is it then, brethren? Whenever you come together, each of you has a psalm, has a teaching, has a tongue, has a revelation, has an interpretation"* (1 Corinthians 14:26 NKJV). What was lacking was that they did not *"discern the Lord's body"* (1 Corinthians 11:29 NKJV). To discern the body and blood of Christ requires some understanding of the context of the meal, and to know what Jesus taught on the subject.

In this booklet we shall look at:

i)   The meaning of the Passover;
ii) The teaching of Jesus on bread and wine;
iii) The teaching of Paul;
iv) The meaning of the bread and wine for Christians.

8

2

The Meaning of
The Passover

Jesus was, of course, steeped in the history of His people. When He sat down to eat that last meal with His 12 closest friends, it had a poignancy for Him which they couldn't have guessed at, as He was about to become the culmination of centuries of history – indeed, of eternity's most ancient plans. We have all seen artists' impressions of the Last Supper. They usually portray Jesus and the Twelve reclining on couches around the table on which the supper stands. John is shown leaning his head upon Jesus, and very often Judas is shown opposite Jesus, where eye contact during the meal becomes unavoidable, as if to emphasise Paul's words that Jesus gave them the bread and wine on the **same** night on which He was betrayed. But how did Jesus view the proceedings?

He would have had in His mind a vivid picture of all that the Passover elements on the table stood for. Passover was the feast by which the Jewish people commemorated (and still do) how God delivered them from bondage in Egypt. The word Passover comes from the Hebrew "pesach" meaning to pass over, as in *"and when I see the blood I will pass over you"*(Exodus 12:13 NKJV).

For 430 years the children of Israel had been in slavery in Egypt. God had prepared Moses to bring them out into freedom and a land of their own. There had been many confrontations between the occult powers of the Egyptians and the power of God through Moses. Despite all the evidence of God's power, Pharaoh refused to let the children of Israel go. God's final judgement was to kill all the first-born sons in the land of Egypt (Exodus 12:29-30). To escape this judgement, each family of the children of Israel took a perfect lamb from the flock on the tenth day of the first month. On the fourteenth day at twilight they slaughtered the lamb and daubed its blood on the lintels and doorposts of their homes (Exodus 12:1-14).

They roasted the lamb and ate it at night with unleavened bread and bitter herbs, with their outer clothes fastened at the waist, their sandals on their feet and their staffs in their hands. In this way they were ready to leave as soon as Pharaoh let them go.

From then on, all generations of Jewish people were to celebrate the Passover until the end of time. It was to be part of the Fast of Unleavened Bread, which lasted for seven days and overlapped the Passover. On the 13th day of the month of Nisan, all leaven had to be removed from the house and none allowed in until the 21st day (Exodus 12:15, 12:19; 13:7). The Passover meal was celebrated on the 15th day. The unleavened bread was to remind the Israelites of their hurried departure from Egypt. The bitter herbs, eaten with the bread, were to remind them of the bitterness of slavery. The roast lamb was to remind them of the lambs whose blood had marked out their homes and that had protected them, as the angel of death passed over them and killed the first-born of the Egyptians. *"So shall this day be to you a memorial; and you shall keep it as a feast to the Lord throughout your generations"*(Exodus 12:14).

A description of the Passover

There is a book entitled 'The Haggadah' (a Hebrew word meaning 'the telling') which gives detailed instructions of how the Passover was to be celebrated. In *"The Story of Christ"*, Giovani Papini describes it in this way: "The Passover of the Israelites is but a feast in memory of their deliverance out of Egypt. That victorious flight from an abject state of bondage, accompanied as it had been by so much that was miraculous, and made possible by the openly manifested favour of the Almighty, has never been forgotten by a people destined, nevertheless, again to bear the yoke of slavery and to submit to the same of other deportations. In perpetual memory of this precipitous Exodus an annual festival was instituted that took the name of the Passover –

Pesach – Easter. It consisted of a sort of banquet that symbolised the hasty repasts of the fugitives. A lamb or kid was cooked in the quickest way which was roasted before the fire. Bread was baked without yeast, for there was no time to wait for the dough to rise. They must eat in haste, staff in hand, with their loins already girded and shoes upon their feet, as if they were to set forth on a journey.

The bitter herbs represent the coarse, wild vegetables the fugitives snatched by the way to still the pangs of hunger on that pilgrimage. The reddish sauce wherein they dip their bread is to remind them of the bricks the Jewish slaves had been forced to make for Pharaoh. The wine is an addition; it represents the joy of escape, the promise of the longed-for vine, the intoxication of gratitude to the Almighty."

The Haggadah raises the question of the bitter herbs. *"This bitter herb – why do we eat it? Because the Egyptians embittered the lives of our ancestors in Egypt as it is said, 'and they embittered their lives with hard labour in mortar and brick and in all manner of labour in their field; all their labour was imposed on them with rigor'"* (Exodus 1:14). These words help us to understand the element of celebration, the freedom, the gratitude that was part of the Passover meal and which we are to enjoy in the Lord's supper.

The meal was a demonstration

It was to be eaten *"in haste"* (Exodus 12:11 NIV); not necessarily quickly, but *"with your cloak tucked into your belt, your sandals on your feet, and your staff in your hand."* This was a demonstration that they were on a journey of deliverance from slavery into the land of their inheritance.

When He celebrated the Passover meal that night, Jesus knew something that His disciples would understand much later. The short journey He was about to make from the Mount of Olives to the hill of Calvary was to be the journey which would take His people, all those who were to be *"in Christ"*, whom Paul would one day describe as having been *"crucified with Christ"*

11

(Galatians 2:20) out of the bondage of slavery of Satan, into *"the glorious freedom of the children of God"* (Romans 8:21 NIV), *"out of the power of darkness and into the Kingdom of the Son of His love"* (Colossians 1:13 NKJV).

The meal was a permanent custom

This day was to be observed throughout all generations as an everlasting ordinance (Exodus 12:17). The meal was to be a constant reminder to all generations of their deliverance. This was so important that God reminded them of the details of His instructions concerning the Passover twice more (Numbers 9:1-5, Deuteronomy 16:1-8). In the same way, when Jesus instituted the Lord's Supper, He intended that His people should not simply remember His death in some morbid meal resembling a wake, but celebrate the freedom and enjoy the benefits that He has given to His people by His triumphant victory on the cross.

The meal was symbolic

Can you imagine what must have been going through Jesus' mind as He shared the Passover lamb with His disciples? They knew that John had referred to Him as *"the Lamb of God, who takes away the sin of the world"* (John 1:29, 36, see also Acts 8:32). But they had probably never stopped to consider what this meant. For Jesus, it meant that the full horror of what He had been born for was now almost upon Him. But there must also have been a joy at doing His Father's will, and a tremendous sense that everything which the Passover lamb had symbolised to the Jewish people for so many centuries was about to reach its fulfilment in Him. Just as the sacrificial blood had averted the wrath of God from the homes of the Israelites, so He was about to avert God's wrath from humankind. Just as the slaughter of the lambs had meant life to the Children of Israel, so now His death was to bring life to the world. The Lord Jesus is described by Isaiah as one who *"did not open His mouth; He was led like a lamb to the slaughter, and as a sheep before her shearers is silent, so He did not open His mouth"* (Isaiah 53:7 NIV). In 1 Corinthians 5:7 Jesus is described as *"Christ our Passover"* (NKJV) and *"Christ our Paschal lamb"* (RSV). The instructions for the Passover Lamb were clear. None of its bones shall be broken (Exodus 14:26). The Psalmist prophesied of the Lord Jesus *"He guards all his bones, not one of them is broken"* (Psalm 34:20), and even after death Jesus' bones were not broken (John 19:36).

This Passover Lamb was not a lamb taken from the flock, he was *"the Son of God, the Lamb of God that takes away the sin of the world"* (John 1:29). He too was without blemish for He was tempted *"in all points as we are, yet without sin"* (Hebrews 4:15).

So this was the background against which Jesus ate a Passover meal with His friends. He also instituted a new feast. This was a 'New Covenant' meal (Luke 22:20). A celebration not of a Passover of history but a celebration of new life, of new beginnings in Christ.

This meal was to be known to the early church as the "Eucharist" (from a Greek word, *eucharisteo*, to give thanks), or as the "Love Feast" (from a Greek word, *agape*, love), and as the "Lord's Supper". Just as the Jews had remembered and celebrated their deliverance and their inheritance, so the followers of Jesus would now remember and celebrate the freedom they have in Him.

3

The Teaching of Jesus
on Bread and Wine

Jesus spoke of His body and His blood on that night when He was betrayed. *"And as they were eating, Jesus took bread, blessed it and broke it and gave it to the disciples and said, 'Take, eat, this is my body.' Then he took the cup and gave thanks and gave it to them, saying, 'Drink from it, all of you, for this is my blood of the New Covenant."* (Matthew 26:26, 27). It was not the first time that He had taught His disciples about His flesh and His blood. What had happened was this: Jesus had said that He was the bread which came down from heaven, and had spoken about this at some length. *"'I am the bread of life. Your forefathers ate the manna in the wilderness, and are dead. This is the bread which comes down from heaven, that one may eat of it and not die. I am the living bread which came down from heaven. If anyone eats of this bread, he will live forever; and the bread that I shall give is My flesh, which I shall give for the life of the world.' The Jews therefore quarrelled among themselves, saying, 'How can this man give us His flesh to eat?'*

"Then Jesus said to them, 'Most assuredly, I say to you, unless you eat the flesh of the Son of Man and drink His blood, you have no life in you. Whoever eats My flesh and drinks My blood has eternal life, and I will raise him up at the last day. For My flesh is food indeed, and My blood is drink indeed. He who eats My flesh and drinks My blood abides in Me and I in him. As the living Father sent me, and I live because of the Father, so he who feeds on Me will live because of Me. This is the bread which came down from heaven – not as your fathers ate the manna, and are dead. He who eats this bread will live forever'" (John 6:48-58 NKJV).

This caused a dispute with the Jewish leaders. They found this teaching so abhorrent and controversial (especially to a race into whose consciousness had been instilled a ceremonial law forbidding the consumption of blood) that many of His followers took offence and left Him.

"Then Jesus said to the twelve, 'Do you also want to go away?' Then Simon Peter answered Him, 'Lord to whom shall we go? You have the words of eternal life. Also, we have come to believe and know that You are the Christ, the Son of the living God'" (John 6:67-69 NKJV). And it was in this context, at the moment when He gave the first teaching about His body and blood being the only source of eternal life, that Jesus spoke these words: *"Have I not chosen you, the Twelve? Yet one of you is a devil!"* and John added, *"He meant Judas, the son of Simon Iscariot, who, though one of the Twelve, was later to betray Him"* (John 6:70 NIV). Even at this stage of His life and ministry, when the cross was still some time away, Jesus could not speak of His flesh and blood without reflecting that Judas would betray Him to the authorities for His body to be broken and His blood spilt as an atonement for sin.

Clearly, Jesus did not mean that people would literally eat His flesh and drink His blood. The bread and wine were to be symbols of His flesh and blood. Over the centuries there have been varying ideas about what Jesus meant, and it is worth taking a brief look at what the church has sometimes taught.

4

A Historical
Perspective

At one time, the church's teaching was that by a divine miracle enacted on the bread and wine, these elements turned into the actual flesh and blood of Jesus. Radbertus was Abbott of Corby from 884-851 AD, and it was he who first formed this doctrine which became known as "transubstantiation". Radbertus maintained that once a priest had spoken words of consecration over the bread and wine, no trace of bread or wine remained in these elements, but what remained was actually and corporally the blood and body of Jesus Christ. This became the unchallenged teaching of the church until the time of the reformation in Europe in the early 16th century. At that time the Holy Spirit moved in such a way that in Holland, Germany and England, some of the finest scholars of the day began to have a hunger for the Word of God. By reading it, many of them were born again, and began to compare the teaching of the church with the teaching of the Bible. In many points the church was found sadly wanting.

The doctrine of transubstantiation had two important implications in the lives of ordinary churchgoers. Firstly, because the eucharist elements were believed (despite all obvious appearances to the contrary) to have become literally and corporally the body and blood of Jesus Himself, and no longer in any way bread or wine, they were worshipped as if they were Christ Himself. Thus, everyone who attended the mass took part in a weekly act of idolatry. Secondly, as the body and blood of Christ, they were offered at every mass as a sacrifice for sin. In this way, the church was denying that Christ's once-for-all death on the cross had been a full, perfect and final atonement for sin, or that people could be saved by putting their faith in what Christ had accomplished on their behalf on the cross. It denied the need to be born again, and insisted instead that salvation depended on attendance at this weekly sacrifice in atonement for sin, as well as other observances.

The martyrs who were put to death during the time of the Reformation (over three hundred of them in this country) died in defence of the doctrine that salvation comes through faith in Jesus Christ alone. They were all judged on one simple question.

"I was asked whether I believed in the sacrament to be the very body and blood of our Saviour Christ that was born of the Virgin Mary, and hanged on the cross, really and substantially? I answered, 'I think it to be false. I cannot understand really and substantially to signify otherwise than corporally. But corporally Christ is only in heaven, and so Christ cannot be corporally in your sacrament.' And therefore he was condemned and burned." (*Light From Old Times* by J.C. Ryle, p.41).

Thomas Cranmer answered the same question in these words, "They say that Christ is corporally under or in the form of bread and wine. We say that Christ is not there, neither corporally nor spiritually; but in them that worthily eat and drink the bread and wine He is spiritually; and corporally in heaven." (ibid., p.54) He, too, was martyred for it, but not before he had succeeded in establishing this principle in the 39 articles of faith on which the Church of England was founded:

"Transubstantiation (or the change of the substance of Bread and Wine) in the Supper of the Lord, cannot be proved by Holy Writ: but is repugnant to the plain words of Scripture, overthroweth the nature of a sacrament, and hath given occasion to many superstitions. The Body of Christ is given, taken and eaten, in the Supper, only after a heavenly and spiritual manner. And the means whereby the Body of Christ is received and eaten in the Supper is Faith. The sacrament of the Lord's Supper was not, by Christ's ordinance, carried about, lifted up, or worshipped." (The 28th Article of the Church of England, taken from the Book of Common Prayer.)

5

Six Benefits of the
Bread and Wine

Whilst the bread and wine are not changed into the literal body and blood of Jesus, Jesus did teach that just as food and drink are digested and give strength to the one who has eaten it, so those who eat the bread and drink the wine and clearly accept that they are symbols of His body and blood, would receive real benefits. *"For My flesh is food indeed and My blood is drink indeed"* (John 6:55). The eating and drinking in themselves show the believer that he is taking into his own being all the life of Christ.

In this passage, Jesus lists six benefits of "eating His flesh and drinking His blood."

● **We will have life in us…** *"Most assuredly I say to you, unless you eat the flesh of the Son of Man and drink His blood you have no life in you"* (John 6:53).

● **We will have resurrection life and be raised up at the last day…** *"Whoever eats My flesh and drinks My blood has eternal life and I will raise him up at the last day"* (John 6:54).

● **We will be strengthened…** *"For My flesh is food indeed and My blood is drink indeed"* (John 6:55).

● **We will know what it is to abide in Jesus…** *"He who eats My flesh and drinks My blood abides in Me and I in him"* (John 6:56).

● **We will know the life of Christ within us…** *"He who feeds on Me will live because of Me"* (John 6:57).

● **We will have eternal life...** *"He who eats this bread will live forever"* (John 6:58).

The New Covenant

Let us now return to the scene in the upper room where Jesus sat eating that last Passover meal with His twelve disciples – a meal of which He said, *"With fervent desire I have desired to eat this Passover with you before I suffer"* (Luke 22:15 NKJV). All the gospels describe this meal in their own way (Matthew 26:17-30, Mark 14:12-26, Luke 22:14-23 and John 13:18-20). Each of them emphasises different aspects of it; for example, John has much to say about Jesus washing the disciple's feet, and about the dipping of the bread by Judas and Jesus as a sign that Judas was the one to betray Him. But there are some features of the story which are common to all the gospels, and these are the things which show us what Jesus was seeking to teach His disciples.

● In breaking the bread, Jesus was demonstrating dramatically, in a way that His disciples were never likely to forget, that it was a symbol of His Body broken for them.

● When He took the cup, filled with red wine, and gave it to His disciples, He was telling them – again in the clear, pictorial way which they would always remember – that it represented the establishing of a new covenant in His blood. This new covenant had been promised through the prophet Jeremiah: *"The time is coming, declares the Lord, when I will make a new covenant with the house of Israel and with the house of Judah. It will not be like the covenant I made with their forefathers when I took them by the hand to lead them out of Egypt, because they broke My covenant, though I was a husband to them, declares the Lord. This is the covenant that I will make with the house of Israel after that time, declares the Lord. I will put My law in their minds and write it on their hearts. I will be their God and they will be My people. No longer will a man teach his neighbour, or a man his brother, saying, 'Know the Lord,' because they will all know Me, from the least of them to the greatest, declares the Lord. For I will forgive their wickedness and remember their sins no more"* (Jeremiah 31:31-34 NIV).

● Jesus gave them the cup not only as a reminder of the New Covenant, but also to be a symbol of His blood which was to be shed for the forgiveness of sins, just as it says in Hebrews 9-22, *"Without the shedding of blood there is no forgiveness"* (NIV).

● Jesus gave them the cup with a reminder of a future kingdom. *"But I say to you, I will not drink of this fruit of the wine from now on until that day I drink it new with you in My Father's kingdom"* (Matthew 26:29 NKJV). Luke records that Jesus said more about the kingdom after He had passed the cup to His disciples: *"I bestow upon you a kingdom, just as My Father bestowed one upon Me, that you may eat and drink at My table in My kingdom and sit on thrones judging the twelve tribes of Israel"* (Luke 22:30 NKJV).

In Luke's record of the events, he refers to two cups: *"Then He took the cup and gave thanks and said, 'Take this and divide it among yourselves.'... Likewise He also took the cup after supper, saying, 'This cup is the new covenant in My blood, which is shed for you'"* (Luke 22:17, 20 NKJV). The Passover meal actually involved the drinking of four cups of wine: the cup of sanctification, the cup of the celebration of the lamb, the cup of thanksgiving and the cup with closing prayers.

Both Matthew and Mark recall that after the meal Jesus and the disciples sang a hymn (Matthew 26:30, Mark 14:26). This hymn, part of Passover meal, was the great "Hallel" based on Psalms 114-118. The instructions were that it should be sung to a "rollicking melody". Part of the words were: *"If He had only brought us out of Egypt and afflicted judgement on the Egyptians it would have sufficed... how much then do we have to thank Him, for all the blessings conferred upon us by the Almighty. He supplied us with everything in the wilderness. He gave us the Sabbath and led us to Sinai and gave us the Law. He led us into the land and gave us the holy temple."*

What significance these words must have had for Jesus, who

knew just how much more God was about to do, not only for His people, but for all who would accept it, Jews and Gentiles. He was about to bring them out of the kingdom of darkness and into the inheritance of the saints in the kingdom of light (Colossians 1:12-13). He was about to make available to them the supply of all their needs forever by His glorious riches in Christ Jesus (Philippians 4:20). He was about to bring them into a permanent state of holiness which would be for them a Sabbath rest (Hebrews 4:1-11). His law, as we have already seen, was to be written on their hearts (Jeremiah 31:33), since He would give them a new nature whose natural tendency was to do what His Spirit desires (Romans 8:5-6). And He was no longer to live in temples made with hands, but He was to live in His people themselves, and they would be temples for His Spirit (1 Corinthians 6:19). So, *"for the joy that was set before Him"*(Hebrews 12:2 NKJV). He was able to sing that cheerful song even as He stared into the jaws of the dreadful death He was about to undergo.

6

The Teachings
of Paul

Paul's teachings about bread and wine are found in three main passages; 1 Corinthians 5:6-13, 1 Corinthians 10:14-22 and 1 Corinthians 11:17-34. We shall examine each passage.

1 Corinthians 5

> *"Your boasting is not good. Don't you know that a little yeast works through the whole batch of dough? Get rid of the old yeast, that you may be a new batch without yeast – as you really are. For Christ, our Passover Lamb has been sacrificed. Therefore let us keep the festival, not with the old yeast, the yeast of malice and wickedness, but with bread without yeast, the bread of sincerity and truth. I have written to you in my letter not to associate with sexually immoral people – not at all meaning the people of this world who are immoral, or the greedy and swindlers, or idolaters. In that case you would have to leave this world. But now I am writing to you that you must not associate with anyone who calls himself a brother but is sexually immoral or greedy, an idolater or a slanderer, a drunkard or a swindler. With such a man do not even eat. What business is it of mine to judge those outside the church? Are you not to judge those inside? God will judge those outside. Expel the wicked man from among you."* (1 Corinthians 5:6-13 NIV)

Some of our Sunday papers – the kind that love to gloat over stories of religious people coming morally unstuck – would have had a field-day with the church in Corinth. This church had a

23

problem concerning sexual immorality – and of a kind that made even the pagans gasp. A man was sleeping with his father's wife. This immorality was no secret in the church, but it was either tolerated or possibly even celebrated as an expression of their freedom in Christ.

In our parents' and grandparents' generations, sexual immorality in the church was probably quite a rarity – or at the least pretty well hidden. But we live in an age when the spirit of the world is sadly infecting the church in many ways. The world says that personal morality is a matter of private concern, and that there is nothing wrong with cohabitation outside of marriage, as well as many other practices which the Bible clearly condemns. To regard any immoral practice that does not apparently harm other people as wrong is thought of as "intolerant" or even "unchristian". As Paul says, what the world does is not for us to judge. But when there are whole movements within the church which exist to promulgate certain kinds of immorality, as is now the case, it is high time for us to take a fresh look at 1 Corinthians 5.

Paul addresses this issue by calling for the exile of the immoral man from the church, and his deliverance to Satan (1 Corinthians 5:1-5). That dealt with the man, but Paul now has to deal with a church that would tolerate that kind of behaviour and even glory in it (v.6). He refers to the Passover and the feast of Unleavened Bread (v.7).

As we have seen, the feast of the Passover was part of the feast of Unleavened Bread. The instructions were clear, *"Seven days you shall eat unleavened bread. On the first day you shall remove leaven from your houses. For whoever eats leavened bread from the first day until the seventh day, that person shall be cut off from Israel"* (Exodus 12:15), and involved the removing of leaven from houses and land (Deuteronomy 16:4). Paul is referring to leaven and its effect upon bread. He says this is like the effect that this immorality is having upon the church. *"Don't you know that a little yeast works through the whole batch of dough?"* (v.6). In other words, the impurity in one member affects and (if it is tolerated by the church) infects the whole church.

The feast must only be kept when immorality and other

24

behaviour, which Paul outlines in verse 11 as fornication, covetousness, idolatry, abusiveness, drunkenness and threatening behaviour is judged by the church. On a more positive side, sharing then is a real love of life together and a real serving of one another. Only then can the feast be in sincerity and truth.

7

1 Corinthians 10

"Therefore, my beloved, shun the worship of idols. I speak as to sensible men; judge for yourselves what I say. The cup of blessing which we bless, is it not a participation in the blood of Christ? The bread which we break, is it not a participation in the body of Christ? Because there is one bread, we who are many are one body, for we all partake of the same loaf. Consider the practice of Israel; are not those who eat the sacrifices partners in the altar? What do I imply then? That food offered to idols is anything, or that an idol is anything? No, I imply that what pagans sacrifice they offer to demons and not to God. I do not want you to be partners with demons. You cannot drink the cup of the Lord and the cup of demons. You cannot partake at the table of the Lord and the table of demons. Shall we provoke the Lord to jealousy? Are we stronger then He?"

(1 Corinthians 10:14-22, RSV)

On market day in Corinth you might well have seen the same people who had been sharing the Lord's Supper on the first day of the week, now vying with one another to buy food which had been offered to idols. On other occasions, you might have found them eating meals with unbelievers who had bought such meat. And if you had looked into the pagan temples, you would even have seen members of the church attending the feast-days of other gods, because of their supposed freedom in Christ. Paul has already addressed this issue in 1 Corinthians 8:1-13, but now he sets the whole matter in the context of the communion, and so lays down guidelines for the Lord's Supper. This is what he says.

A cup of blessing

"The cup of blessing which we bless, is it not the communion of the blood of Christ? The bread which we break, is it not the communion of the body of Christ?" (1 Corinthians 10:16 NKJV). Paul clearly indicates here that the cup of blessing is a blessing to us as we drink it. It reminds us that Jesus was made a curse for us so that the blessing of Abraham would come upon us (Galatians 3:13-14). It reminds us that as we are identified with Christ, we are *"blessed with every spiritual blessing in the heavenly places in Christ"*(Ephesians 1:3). And so as we participate in the body and blood of the Lord, we in turn bless Him for all that He has done for us, symbolised in the bread and wine.

A communion in the blood and body of Christ

The cup of blessing and the broken bread is a communion in the body and blood of Christ. The word "communion" means a sharing, a participation, a fellowship. This means that as we drink the wine and eat the bread we are sharing and participating in all that Jesus' broken body and poured-out blood has done for us – not simply a past historical event, but something which will always continue to have an ongoing impact on our lives.

This sharing is not only an identification but a oneness with the body and blood of Christ. The word communion, i.e. a "common union", is a word of intimacy, of closeness, referring to the oneness or joining of the believer with the Lord Jesus. Paul uses similar terms, though not the same word, in the context of the sexual union. He says, *"he who joins himself to a harlot is one body with her... but he who is joined to the Lord is one spirit with Him"* (1 Corinthians 6:16-17 NKJV).

This union means that all of the benefits of Christ's **life, death, resurrection** and **ascension** flow to us because we are joined to the Lord Jesus.

By His **life**, Jesus enacted all that is in the heart of God. He made it plain that God's desire for all men is wholeness, healing, happiness and holiness. He demonstrated all these by His life, and

He died to make them available to us. Whenever we celebrate the Lord's Supper, signifying that we are joined to Him, we are affirming the life that He lived, and that we are allowing Him by His Spirit to live His life in us.

By His **death**, Jesus saved us from our sins – the thing which the angel Gabriel told Mary at the Annunciation that He would do. He saved us from the guilt of our sin. From the moment that we put our faith in His atoning work on the cross, no matter what we have done, God no longer accounts us guilty. He also saved us from the power of sin. All those ungodly habits that we have been powerless to overcome begin to lose their dominion over us from the moment we are born again. And He saved us from the penalty of our sin. We will no longer be required to bear the punishment – eternal death – which our sins deserve. All this we are celebrating in this act of remembrance.

By His **resurrection** Jesus gave us a complete certainty of our own resurrection. *"If only for this life we have hope in Christ, we are to be pitied more than all men. But Christ has indeed been raised from the dead, the first fruits of those who have fallen asleep. For since death came through a man, the resurrection of the dead comes also through a man. For as in Adam all die, so in Christ all will be made alive"* (1 Corinthians 15:19-22 NIV). The result of this is that we are free from man's age-old fear of death: *"Since the children have flesh and blood, He too shared in their humanity so that by His death He might destroy him who holds the power of death – that is, the devil – and free those who all their lives were held in slavery by their fear of death."* (Hebrews 2:14-15 NIV). By our communion in the body and blood of the Lord Jesus, we enjoy this great benefit also.

When He **ascended** Jesus took again His rightful place in heaven, and as a direct result, the Holy Spirit was poured out on His church. *"Exalted to the right hand of God, He has received from the Father the promised Holy Spirit and has poured out what you now see and hear... The promise is for you and your children and for all who are far off – for all whom the Lord our God shall call"* (Acts 2:33, 39 NIV). *"When He ascended on high, He led captivity captive and gave gifts to men"* (Ephesians 4:8 NKJV). All that we have received of the Holy Spirit in our individual lives and corporately, and all the gifts and ministries that God has provided for His church, stem from the ascension of the Lord Jesus. This, too, is what we are taking hold of when we participate in the body and blood of the Lord Jesus.

Unity of the Body

The broken bread speaks of the unity of the body: *"Because there is one loaf, we, who are many, are one body, for we all partake of the one loaf"* (1 Corinthians 10:17 NIV). An important part of discerning the body is not only to receive the life and communion of Christ but to receive and recognise the life that is in the Body of Christ, the Church, and to appreciate other believers as members of that Body. This means:

● That we appreciate and accept one another as members of the Body of Christ (1 Corinthians 12:12-31).

● That we give honour to the weaker members of the Body (1 Corinthians 12:22).

● That we recognise and appreciate each other's gifts and ministries (1 Corinthians 12:18).

● That we maintain fellowship by walking in the light with one another (1 John 1:5-9).

● That we serve one another (John 13:15).

● That we recognise that we can draw the life of God from the Body as we are joined to the other members. Paul explains it to the Ephesian church, *"From Him the whole body, joined and held together by every supporting ligament, grows and builds itself up in love, as each part does its work"* (Ephesians 4:16 NIV).

● That we do all we can to serve the Body, to build it up by using the gifts that God has given to us (1 Corinthians 14:1).

● That we recognise both the joys and sorrows of those in the Body (1 Corinthians 12:26).

This means being sensitive to one another. We rejoice with those who are blessed and rejoicing. By practical service, spiritual gifts and sharing our goods, we seek to meet the needs of any who are in need. This is clearly seen in the early church: *"All the believers were one in heart and mind. No one claimed that any of his possessions was his own, but they shared everything they had... There were no needy persons among them. For from time to time those who owned lands or houses sold them, brought the money from the sales and put it at the apostles' feet and it was distributed to anyone as he had need"* (Acts 4:32-35 NIV).

8

1 Corinthians 11

"Now in giving these instructions I do not praise you, since you come together not for the better but for the worse. For first of all when you come together as a church, I hear that there are divisions among you, and in part I believe it. For there must also be factions among you, that those who are approved may be recognised among you. Therefore when you come together in one place, it is not to eat the Lord's Supper. For in eating, each one takes his own supper ahead of others, and one is hungry and another is drunk. What! Do you not have houses to eat and drink in? Or do you despise the church of God and shame those who have nothing? What shall I say to you? Shall I praise you in this? I do not praise you. For I received from the Lord that which I also delivered to you: that the Lord Jesus, on the same night in which He was betrayed took bread; and when He had given thanks He broke it and said, 'Take, eat, this is My body which is broken for you; do this in remembrance of Me.' In the same manner He also took the cup after supper, saying, 'This cup is the new covenant in My blood. This do, as often as you drink it, in remembrance of Me.' For as often as you eat this bread and drink this cup, you proclaim the Lord's death till He comes. Therefore whoever eats this bread or drinks this cup of the Lord in an unworthy manner will be guilty of the body and blood of the Lord. But let a man examine himself and so let him eat of that bread and drink of that cup. For he who eats and drinks in an unworthy manner eats and drinks judgement on himself, not discerning the Lord's body. For this reason many are weak and sick among you and many sleep. For if we would judge ourselves we would not be

judged. But when we are judged, we are chastened by the Lord, that we may not be condemned with the world. Therefore, my brethren, when you come together to eat, wait for one another. But if anyone is hungry, let him eat at home, lest you come together for judgement. And the rest I will set in order when I come." (1 Corinthians 11:17-34 NKJV)

One thing Paul wants to make clear: he didn't invent his doctrine (as some modern New Testament scholars would like us to believe), nor did he crib it from those who'd been Christians before him. No, he learned it by revelation from Christ Himself. He explains what he means by this in greater detail elsewhere.

"I want you to know, brothers, that the gospel I preached is not something that man made up. I did not receive it from any man, nor was I taught it; rather, I received it by revelation from Jesus Christ. For... when God, who set me apart from birth and called me by his grace, was pleased to reveal his Son in me so that I might preach him among the Gentiles, I did not consult any man, nor did I go up to Jerusalem to see those who were apostles before I was, but I went immediately into Arabia and later returned to Damascus. Then after three years I went up to Jerusalem to get acquainted with Peter and stayed with him fifteen days. I saw none of the other apostles – only James the Lord's brother... Fourteen years later I went up again to Jerusalem, this time with Barnabas... I went in response to a revelation and set before them the gospel that I preach among the Gentiles. But I did this privately to those who seemed to be leaders, for fear that I was running or had run my race in vain." (Galatians 1:11-2.2 NIV)

Paul clearly establishes his apostolic authority as one to whom Christ was revealed and whom Christ taught. In 1 Corinthians 11:23, he states that it was Christ who taught him about the Lord's Supper. The words which are used would have been understood by his first readers as a recognised formula used by teachers at the time: "I delivered to you what I also received..." It signified that something of great importance was being communicated. Paul uses the same formula with even greater emphasis when affirming the literal truth of Christ's physical resurrection from the dead: *"For I delivered to you as of first importance what I also received..."* (1 Corinthians 15:3 RSV).

So when the Church at Corinth received Paul's letter and read the words, *"For I received from the Lord that which I also delivered to you, that the Lord Jesus, on the same night in which He was betrayed, took bread...,"* they would have understood, in a way that is not immediately obvious to modern readers, that Paul was laying special emphasis on something of great importance which he had previously communicated to them and did not wish them to forget. This is what Paul then taught them:

Remembrance of Jesus

The bread and wine is a reminder of the work that Jesus did on the cross. Paul reminds them that Jesus said this meal was to be in remembrance of Him (1 Corinthians 11:24-25).

The bread and wine are symbols of the broken body and the poured-out blood of the Lord Jesus. As we eat and drink them, it is a remembrance of what Jesus has done for us on the cross. We can remind ourselves that His blood was shed for our sins and that the blood of Jesus Christ cleanses us from all sin (1 John 1:7). We can remind ourselves that Jesus took our sins and iniquities in His own body on the tree (1 Peter 2:24); that He Himself took our infirmities and bore our sicknesses (Matthew 8:17) and that *"by His stripes we were healed"* (1 Peter 2:24 NKJV).

Covenant meal

The bread and wine teaches us that it is a covenant meal. Jesus said to His disciples, and later to Paul, *"This cup is the new covenant in My blood."* In the ancient world – and not only among the ancient Jews, but in many cultures – a covenant was not valid until blood had been shed. The shedding of blood sealed the covenant conditions which were agreed between the parties to the covenant. This covenant meal which Jesus instituted reminds us of the new covenant, of which the writer to the Hebrews has this to say, *"Jesus is also Mediator of a better covenant, which was established on better promises"* (Hebrews 8:6 NKJV). This covenant meal reminds us of the new covenant. It tells us that all the new covenant promises and all the blessings that flow from that covenant are ours in Christ. It also tells us that we are inextricably bound to one another in that covenant, and that as members of the Body of Christ, we are committed to each other as much as to Him.

Until He comes

The bread and wine proclaim the Lord's death until He comes. *"For as often as you eat this bread and drink this cup, you proclaim the Lord's death until He comes"* (1 Corinthians 11:26 NKJV). Jesus told His disciples that He would not drink of the fruit of the vine again until He drank it with them in His kingdom, and that He had given them a kingdom (Luke 22:18, 30). This meal is a reminder of the future kingdom that we look forward to, which will be established when the Lord Jesus returns. In this meal we remind ourselves of the glorious return of the Lord Jesus Christ and all that means to us believers eagerly looking for His return. Like Paul, we should be able to say, *"Finally there is laid up for me the crown of righteousness, which the Lord, the righteous Judge, will give to me on that Day, and not only to me but also to all who have loved His appearing"* (2 Timothy 4:8 NKJV).

Discernment of the Body

Paul makes it quite clear that members of the Corinthian church are suffering and are dead because they have failed to discern the Lord's body. They are eating and drinking in an unworthy manner. This was happening for a number of reasons:

● They were unclean. That is, there was 'leaven' of immorality in the church unjudged and unresolved (1 Corinthians 5:6).

● They were in disunity. *"First of all, when you come together as a church, I hear that there are divisions among you... therefore when you come together in one place it is not to eat the Lord's Supper"* (1 Corinthians 11:18, 20 NKJV).

● They did not serve one another. In Corinth, the Lord's Supper was celebrated as part of the "love-feast". Every member would bring some food and they would share a meal together, during the course of which they would break bread and wine. The trouble was that, unlike normal social gatherings where people mixed with their own class, in the church situation rich and poor met together, so that there would be a disparity in the amount of food people brought with them. The rich brought large amounts of food and wine, whilst the poor brought very little. But instead of sharing all the food out, each person ate what he had brought with him, without considering anyone else's needs. So while some sat hungrily watching the rich gorging themselves, others got rip-roaring drunk. Paul's instructions were clear; satisfy your hunger before you leave home (v.34), when you come together to eat, wait for one another (v.33) and don't cause embarrassment to the less well-off (v.21).

● They did not discern the body of Christ. They did not discern that the bread and wine was a sharing in Christ's life and that the bread and wine was symbolic of the body and blood of Christ. They were, in fact, treating it as if it had no more significance than any other meal, and each other as if they owed one another no duty of love and respect – as if they were not all members of the same body, with their interests and wellbeing intricately connected.

Rightly discerning the body

Paul encourages the Corinthian believers to escape judgement by "examining" and "judging" themselves (1 Corinthians 11:28, 31). This doesn't mean an unhealthy, morbid search for sin, but an honest scrutiny of the conscience before God, and a joyful examination and appreciation of all that is meant in taking bread and wine. Where this self-examination reveals personal sin, it doesn't lead us to despair – after all, it is God's mercy and forgiveness that we are celebrating in remembering what the cross of Jesus represents to us.

9

Conclusion

So how do we discern the body and blood of Christ correctly?

We remind ourselves:

● We remind ourselves of the death of the Lord Jesus, of His broken body and poured-out blood and all that means to us as believers in Jesus. We pay close attention to the great salvation and deliverance that we have experienced because of Jesus' death. By instituting this regular remembrance, Jesus was making sure that no one would have any excuse for neglecting or ignoring His remedy for sin. *"We must pay more careful attention, therefore, to what we have heard, so that we do not drift away. For if the message spoken by angels was binding, and every violation and disobedience received its just punishment, how shall we escape if we ignore (NKJV: 'neglect') such a great salvation?"* (Hebrews 2:1-3 NIV). We pay close attention to the great salvation and deliverance that we have experienced because of Jesus' death:
  ● Our deliverance from sin.
  ● Our deliverance from sickness.
  ● Our deliverance from Satan's power.
  ● Our deliverance from Satan's judgement.

● We remind ourselves of the unshakeable kingdom that we are receiving in Christ, and all the benefits of that kingdom, which are ours now and in the future. We reign in life, with dominion over all the power of the enemy (Luke 10:19), and we will one day reign with Jesus in His kingdom (2 Timothy 2:12).

We give thanks:

For the body and blood of Jesus:

● For His life – for His incarnation and the life that He lived out among us during the days of His flesh.

● For having resurrection life – for the fact that the same Spirit which raised Jesus from the dead, living in us, gives His life to our mortal bodies (Romans 8:11).

● For His strength – that no matter how great our own sense of weakness, His grace is always sufficient; and more than that, it is in our own weakness that His strength is perfected (2 Corinthians 12:8-9).

● For abiding in Christ – that He makes it possible for us to remain in Him in exactly the same way as a branch remains in the vine, drawing on the life of the plant and so flourishing and bearing much fruit (John 15:5-8).

● For our life in Christ – that from the moment of our rebirth, we are seated in heavenly places with Christ, experiencing life from His perspective, and our life is hidden with Christ in God (Colossians 3:1-3).

● For eternal life that we have and look forward to – that He promises us that we will never die (John 11:26), and that He has gone to prepare a place for us (John 14:3), so that we will go where He has gone, to live with Him forever.

We receive:

● All the blessings of the New Covenant that are in Christ. The covenant that God established with Moses was conditional on obedience to the law, and was mediated through the priesthood. But in sending His Son to be our high priest, God has made Him the mediator of a better covenant. The chief blessings of this covenant are that we will know God and receive His mercy and forgiveness (Hebrews 8:1-13).

● All the benefits that are a result of Christ's life within us. Paul spoke to the Colossian church of *"the glorious riches of this mystery, which is Christ in you, the hope of glory"* (Colossians 1:27 NIV). Christ's life within us is a mystery full of glorious riches. It is a hope of future glory (and the Greek word for hope signifies a favourable and confident expectation), and it enables us to live our lives here and now *"from one degree of glory to another"* (2 Corinthians 3:18 RSV).

● The fulfilment of God's promises in our lives. All God's promises are made available to us in Jesus, and we take hold of them by confidently affirming "amen" to them. *"For no matter how many promises God has made, they are 'Yes' in Christ. And so through Him the 'Amen' is spoken by us to the glory of God"* (2 Corinthians 1:20 NIV).

● The will of God in our lives and situations. So often we shy away from hearing what God's will is for us, afraid that it is bound to be something unpleasant! But Paul assures us that God's will for us is *"good and acceptable and perfect"* (Romans 12:2 NKJV). In fact, the kingdom of God comes now and is realised in our lives when His will is done on earth just as it is in heaven.

We accept:

● God's judgement in our lives. By participating in the Lord's Supper, we are submitting our own personal lives to God's judgement upon our behaviour and speech, and upon the way we conduct ourselves as individual believers in the world.

● God's judgement on immoral and wrong behaviour within the church. Where those who behave in such a way are unrepentant, leading to their exile from the church community, we accept this judgement because we recognise that the Body of Christ must be pure, or it cannot have fellowship with Christ, who is the Head, since He is pure. A body which is not in communion with its head cannot function, or even remain alive for long!

● God's judgement of hidden words and impure motives that damage the Body of Christ. We cannot rightly discern the Lord's body unless we are prepared to do away with all gossip, malice and other secret prejudices that damage the unity of the Body and hinder the work of the Spirit of God.

We appreciate:

● That we are members of the Body of Christ with a unique function, and that we need other members of the Body. *"Now the body is not made up of one part but of many. If the foot should say, 'Because I am not a hand, I do not belong to the body,' it would not for that reason cease to be part of the body. And if the ear should say, 'Because I am not an eye, I do not belong to the body,' it would not for that reason cease to be part of the body. If the whole body were an eye, where would the sense of hearing be? If the whole body were an ear, where would the sense of smell be? But in fact God has arranged the parts in the body, every one of them as He wanted them to be. If they were all one part, where would the body be? As it is, there are many parts but one body"* (1 Corinthians 12:14-20 NIV). So we do all we can to maintain the unity of the Spirit, to accept our brothers and sisters and restore relationships were necessary.

● That other members have unique gifts and ministries. In particular we look out for and give attention to weaker members of the Body. *"The eye cannot say to the hand, 'I don't need you!' And the head cannot say to the feet, 'I don't need you!' On the contrary, those parts of the body that seem to be weaker are indispensable, and the parts that we think are less honourable are treated with special honour. And the parts that are unpresentable are treated with special modesty, while our presentable parts need no special treatment"* (1 Corinthians 12:21-24 NIV).

● The joys and needs of those members of the Body to which we are joined. We seek to rejoice with those who rejoice and weep with those who weep. *"God has combined the members of the body and has given greater honour to the parts that lacked it, so that there should be no division in the body, but that its parts should have equal concern for each other. If one part suffers, every part suffers with it; if one part is honoured, every part rejoices with it. Now you are the Body of Christ, and each one of you is a part of it"* (1 Corinthians 12:24-27 NIV). Paul is saying something quite radical here. If I cut my hand, the rest of my body doesn't have to pray to God for some sympathy, and then do its best to feel for my hand and make appropriately soothing noises. No! If my hand is hurting, my whole body is out of sorts. Paul is saying that we should expect God's Spirit to work in our hearts until our unity is such that we feel one another's joys and sorrows just as acutely as we would if they were happening to us personally.

● The needs of others in the Body. We seek to meet those needs through love, spiritual gifts and practical service. This is another area where the early church were much more radical than most of us have dared to be, and it goes hand-in-hand with our appreciation of what it means to be part of the Body of Christ. *"They devoted themselves to the apostles' teaching and to the fellowship, to the breaking of bread and to prayer... All the believers were together and had everything in common. Selling their possessions and goods, they gave to anyone as he had need"* (Acts 2:42-44 NIV).

We anticipate:

● The return of the Lord Jesus and the coming of His kingdom. No matter what befalls us, no matter what is shaken to pieces in our own lives or in the world around us, we live as servants of a King whose kingdom is not of this world (John 18:36). Because

His kingdom is unshakeable despite the shaking of everything around us, our response to all the circumstances of our lives is one of thankfulness and reverence towards Jesus, our King of Kings: *"Therefore since we are receiving a kingdom that cannot be shaken, let us be thankful, and so worship God acceptably with reverence and awe, for our God is a consuming fire"* (Hebrews 12:28-29 NIV).

We celebrate:

● After the meal Jesus and His disciples sang a hymn. Despite the sorrow that was coming, there was joy in looking forward. We, too, can celebrate our freedom, our healing, our deliverance, our inheritance and our life in Christ. Because of what He has done, because of His life within us, and because of all that we look forward to, we can do this in remembrance of Him with great joy.

If you have enjoyed this book and would like to help us to send a copy of it and many other titles to needy pastors in the **Third World**, please write for further information or send your gift to:

Sovereign World Trust, P.O. Box 777, Tonbridge, Kent TN11 0ZS, United Kingdom

or to the **'Sovereign World'** distributor in your country.